Latimer Studies 47

BUILDING MULTI-RACIAL CHURCHES

JOHN ROOT

The Latimer Trust

Contents Page

Author's Note

This booklet was originally published in 1994, in part responding to the concerns and initiatives highlighted in 'The Faith in the City' report. It is being republished in 2020 both because of a continuing need for resources for building congregations in multi-ethnic areas, and especially because of the confluence of attention raised by the Black Lives Matter protests, concern over the disproportionate number of deaths to people from ethnic minorities from Covid-19, and the outrageous manifestation of institutional racism towards long-standing but undocumented 'Windrush' migrants from the Caribbean. More than a quarter of a century after its original publication it has a dated feel in some parts, but overall I think it still has a contemporary resonance even with the many developments that have occurred over that period. In particular the writings of theologians such as N T Wright have underlined the centrality of united but diverse multi-ethnic congregations in the life and witness of the church.

Whilst there are only a few minor changes to the text, I hope the addition of a bibliography will also help update the booklet. Readers may note inconsistencies in the use of the words 'racial/ethnic/cultural' but I hope the context provides sufficiently firm ground to cope with the slippery way in which the connotations of words evolve.

John Root

July 2020

Introduction

The Church of England's statements on being an ethnically just and inclusive community consistently run the danger that either they are simply ignored in the parishes, or that they are paid lip service to, but no way is ever found to implement them effectively. This danger is particularly acute when it applies to the church's ministry in areas it has traditionally found difficult, such as big cities. The lack of effective local ministry can be for a time forgotten in a flurry of central committee activity and the expression of worthy sentiments.

But ultimately the credibility of the Church of England's rightful commitment to being a multi-racial church will stand or fall by how far and how effectively it consists of multi-racial parishes.

This booklet is an attempt to map out the sort of convictions and policies that are needed to enable the Church of England to become multi-racial. It applies, therefore, to churches in those areas that are recognised as 'multi-racial'. However, population movements are such that very considerable areas of Britain are now multi-racial – to take an area I know well, they include all of north-west Greater London, and areas that 10 years ago were seen as 'white highlands' are now ethnically mixed. Increasingly this is becoming true of small towns and even rural areas. Further, the issues raised here have importance for national policies, and these will be referred to in passing.

Some definitions are needed at this point. What is meant by 'race' needs careful thought. It has only been used as a word to classify groups of people in the last two centuries, and in that time its meaning has changed.[1] It does not relate neatly to any Old or New Testament concepts. Its present meaning begins from obvious differences of appearance, chiefly skin-colour; but such differences are then extrapolated to more highly charged distinctions, notably of culture or ethnicity on the one hand, and social class or access to power on the other. It is a fact that

---

[1] See Michael Banton, *The Idea of Race*, Tavistock Publications, 1977. 'Both in Britain and France the word "race" starts to change its significance round about the year 1800 ... In the nineteenth century race comes to signify an inherent physical quality', p 18.

these differences, especially those of wealth and power, have been lined up in an approximate way with differences in physical appearance over the last four centuries, that has made race a source of conflict in the modern world.[2]

It is important to bear this use in mind, particularly when we discuss the biblical material in chapter 2. Relationships between people of different coloured skins are not common in scripture, and when they do occur are given very little significance. (The Cushites who married Moses in Numbers 12:1, and who rescued Jeremiah from the cistern in Jeremiah 38:7, would have been dark-skinned.) By contrast, relationships between culturally and ethnically different groups of people on the one hand, and between people with different wealth, power and status on the other hand, are a vital part of both Old and New Testament histories. It is in reflecting on how these differences are treated that we see what discipleship and fellowship mean in a 'multi-racial' world today.

'Ethnic groups' is a firmer and also more biblical term than 'race'. Throughout the bible it is recognised that individuals belong to particular 'peoples', and the term recognises the way in which today we all identify ourselves as belonging to particular groups, though we may need warning to give to others the flexibility and freedom we probably claim for our own ethnic self-identification. Stronger warning is also needed against the misuse of the term 'ethnic' to apply only to non-whites, as though white people had no ethnicity of their own. An Anglican village church may well be as much an 'ethnic church' as an Urdu-speaking gathered urban church, though it is not an ethnic minority church.

'Multicultural' refers to the broad attributes of different ethnic groups, and the way their cultures relate to each other. The word draws attention to much that people find valuable about their own culture, and the enrichment that we are mutually offered. However, over-emphasis on the concept has also been criticised for drawing too much attention to relatively minor differences such as food and dress, and for ignoring

---

[2] See my article on 'Race' in *New Dictionary of Theology* edited by Sinclair B Ferguson & David F Wright, IVP, 1988, pp 555–6.

major issues of how some groups can use greatly superior power to oppress others.[3]

In this booklet I have used the phrase 'multi-racial in membership, leadership and ethos'. I take this to be a broad outline of our goal. A church can hardly be called multi-racial at all if its membership is not multi-racial. Too easily, however, the matter stops there; black people attend but take no greater part in 'owning' the church. This has frequently been identified as the heart of the Church of England's dilemma in multi-racial parishes.[4] Moving to a situation where white people honour the leadership of blacks, and where black people freely exercise the gifts that they have, is a primary challenge for us. Multi-racial in ethos is harder to identify – what it fully means will only appear as our churches move forward, but it warns against a situation where black people are simply grafted on to an unchanging church, and encourages us to look for the contribution of black Christians to produce a variety of new fruits in our churches.

As regards the words used for different ethnic groups, people have a glorious capacity to elude labels, and I will not feel too guilty if they are used imprecisely. The context should normally indicate the meaning. Thus 'black' is used, as in this section, to mean 'non-white' – essentially, those whose roots are in the Caribbean, Africa or Asia. At other times, however, it is used for people of Caribbean or African background, as opposed to Asian, both those born in those places and those whose ancestors came from there. 'West Indian' usually means those who have lived some of their lives in the West Indies. 'Afro-Caribbean' refers to people of African ancestry whose roots are in the Caribbean.

---

[3] See for example Chris Mullard in *Black Britain*, 1973: 'Too much nonsense has been talked about the wrong issues: integration, assimilation, acceptance, immigrant problems, language, customs, dress, and bridge building when the white bank towers several hundred feet above the black one'. Such a position has been held dogmatically by Marxists, for whom cultural relationships were always secondary to economic relationships. But the reality has outlived Marxism!

[4] For example, the experience recorded in, *Seeds of Hope*, General Synod of the Church of England, 1991, 23: 'just creep in for worship and creep back out'.

I. FORMING CONVICTIONS

If a local church is to be multi-racial, it is essential that its leaders are convinced that it is both right and necessary. Failure to be convinced that a local church should reflect the ethnic variety of its neighbourhood or belief that it is theoretically desirable but practically too difficult to be worth giving much effort to, will mean the persistence of basically white 'mono-racial' churches, certainly in leadership and ethos, though perhaps not entirely in membership.

Multi-racial churches, then, can only be built on the conviction that God wills for the church to reflect the ethnic variety of the community and that he intends us to give prayer, thought and energy to bringing it about.

The logic of the gospel is that it is for all people. God's promise to Abraham was that all peoples would be blessed through him. At the low point of Jewish national history in the Babylonian exile, Isaiah 40–55 burns particularly brightly with the conviction that the trajectory of God's purposes goes beyond restoring the people to their land and on to bringing all nations to live by the light of their faith. The picture of all nations coming up to Jerusalem to worship envisaged a social and relational unity, not merely an abstract one.[5] There would be harmony of relationships on the holy mountain.

What understanding of human identity and culture underlay such a vision? Basic was the conviction that all people were made in God's image, and therefore had an inherent value. However, sin means that the culture that humanity produces is ambiguous. The punishment for Adam and Eve's disobedience is that both bearing a family and working the land become painful. The increase in man's cultural potential and the consequent pride leads to the disruption and division of Babel. Culture, then, not only expresses man's dignity and identity, it can also become a barrier against God, which is doomed to frustration. 'Culture' in general is a necessary and valuable expression of our humanness; particular 'cultures' are transient, incomplete and conflicting.

---

[5] It has been pointed out how the hajj promotes the inter-ethnic unity of Islam through just such a literal and physical gathering together of people from different countries in a very small area. See for example Malise Ruthven, *Islam in the Modern World*, Penguin, 1984, 46.

This is a more negative assessment of culture than is common in our society today, where guilt about the damage done to other cultures has led on to a protective over-sensitivity. Whilst acknowledging the value that we all derive from belonging to particular cultures, we are under no mandate to preserve them unchanged. Each culture is different, and in different ways bears the stamp of human aspiration, and of human resistance to God. Practically this means that we are to sit loose to our cultural inheritance (as Paul did to his – Philippians 3:4–9); to gladly draw from the culture of others; yet not to be silenced by the political correctness that insists that cultures should be beyond criticism. Instead as the products of human history they will in varying ways reflect both the glory and the shame of their producers.

Furthermore Babel is now transcended by Pentecost, where God's new creation draws people back together into a Spirit-given unity. Our old cultures are not done away with; we retain some of their characteristics, and look forward to the glory and honour of the nations being brought into the holy city (Revelation 21:26). But our first identity is in the new people of God, where God seeks to redeem and purify our old cultural inheritance, and where we share the riches that each culture has.

Thus the early church both rejoiced in its cultural diversity, and yet subordinated those cultures to life in the new people of God. A multi-cultural band of Gentiles fulfilled Isaiah's prophecy, and brought the church's offering to Jerusalem (Acts 20:4). Luke delights to scatter his text with ethnic details about the members of the early church. In particular the church at Antioch in Acts 13 shows a rich diversity of colour, culture and class: Simeon, a black man; Manaen, a courtier; Barnabas, a wealthy Jew from Cyprus, and Paul from a strictly Jewish background.

Such unity-in-diversity continued to be a leading characteristic of the church as it spread. Writing on Acts, John Stott suggests that in Luke's account of Paul's ministry at Philippi, he chooses three particular conversion stories from many others 'because they demonstrate how God breaks down dividing barriers and can unite in Christ people of very different kinds'.(footnote?) Thus, nationally Lydia was from Asia Minor, the slave girl most likely a local Greek, and the gaoler probably a retired Roman soldier. Socially, Lydia and the slave girl clearly came from opposite poles of the social spectrum, whilst 'the gaoler was socially half-way between the two women'.[6]

Paul's writings constantly speak of how the gospel over-rides all human distinctions. In similar lists, he speaks of how faith in Christ unites across religious/ethnic, social and sexual differences (Galatians 3:28), and across ethnic, religious, cultural and social differences (Colossians 3:11). Thus in Ephesians 2:19, 20, the church that is 'built on the foundation of the apostles and prophets, with Jesus Christ himself as the chief cornerstone' is specifically one in which once excluded people are 'no longer foreigners and aliens'.

All of this foreshadows the glorious vision of Revelation (7:9) when worship and praise is given to 'our God ... and to the Lamb' by 'a great multitude that no-one could count, from every nation, tribe, people and language'. Those of us who worship in multi-racial churches have the joy of a foretaste of that.

It is quite alien to the Bible's understanding of truth to believe that these can be 'spiritual' or 'eternal' realities which can for the moment be laid aside in practice. What is true of the age to come, is to be lived out here and now. If the church is the new creation, the body of the first-born from the dead, then the church must be here and now the place where old divisions of race, culture and class are over-ridden by the new reality of life together in Christ.

For this reason the first Christians took pains to give reality to their multi-racial unity. We should not under-estimate the cost to them of this. The Jewish sense of a unique and separate identity was massive. Thus at key points self-conscious decisions had to be made to ensure that the early churches did not fall into being 'homogenous units' that conformed to existing ethnic divisions. One such key point is recorded in Acts 6, verses 1 to 6, where ethnic tensions arose in the church in Jerusalem between Greek and Aramaic speaking Jewish Christians, because widows in the former group were being overlooked in the distribution of food. The distinction between the two groups, John Stott writes, 'must go beyond origin and language to culture ... There had, of course always been rivalry between these groups in Jewish culture; the tragedy is that it was perpetuated within the new community of Jesus who by his death had

---

[6] John Stott, *The Message of Acts* (The Bible Speaks Today series), IVP, 1990, 262, 268–9.

abolished such distinctions' (pp 120–1). If, on the one hand, the Twelve saw the need not to be distracted from their primary work of prayer and preaching by such conflicts, neither did they see the matter as too trivial to bother with, nor as evidence that the two groups 'couldn't get on' and were best left to go their separate ways. Rather they exercised their leadership by taking the problem seriously; by devising an imaginative and practical solution to the problem, that took the needs of the 'outsider' group seriously; and delegated it to wise and Sprit-filled men to implement.

The creation of the seven 'deacons' in Acts 6, has much to say to churches in all multi-ethnic situations. It reminds us that attitudes derived from this passing age will remain with us to create tensions in our churches. Our response is to be neither apathy nor despair, but should be an amalgam of spiritual discernment and practical wisdom that creates specific solutions to these tensions. As history unfolds there are a myriad of new possibilities for inter-ethnic tension; in each case we should be looking to God for the wisdom to create adequate responses that preserve the visible and practised inter-ethnic unity of the church. In all of this, one important point to learn from the Jerusalem church was its instinct to give power to those who felt excluded; thus all seven deacons had Greek names and probably came from the Greek-speaking Jewish community that had seen itself as disadvantaged in the food distribution.

The first Christians were neither so godly as to be free of ethnic tensions, nor so 'spiritual' as to consider practical strategies for solving them to be too trivial. Being part of a multi-racial church today will raise tensions at times; we should not grudge the effort, nor despise the apparently small-scale 'parish pump' activities, that are needed to handle them constructively.

As the gospel spread beyond the Jewish community the tensions became considerably greater. We can scarcely imagine the change of heart required for Peter to witness to Cornelius, and for him to learn to 'make no distinction' (RSV translation of Acts 11:12 *meden diakrinanta*); that, as Stott quotes Bengel's commentary, God 'is not indifferent of religions but indifferent of nations'.[7] When the Council of Jerusalem met to discuss the terms on which Gentiles could be admitted to church

---

[7] Op cit, pp 187, 190.

membership, we see this concern to maintain a lived-out unity of Jewish and Gentile believers. Four prohibitions were imposed on Gentile believers: 'from food sacrificed to idols, from blood, from the meat of strangled animals and from sexual immorality' (Acts 15:29) – the latter probably meaning the marriages of blood relationship in Leviticus 18. They all referred to ceremonial prohibitions and were intended not to cause offence to Jewish believers, particularly, it has been suggested, in the intimacy of the eucharistic fellowship meal.[8] Adjustments, then, were to be made on both sides. On the one hand Jewish believers needed to break free from deeply ingrained habits of thought that caused them to feel inordinately superior to Gentiles, meanwhile Gentile believers were to be sensitive to the traditions of their Jewish fellow-believers, and not cause needless difficulties for them. Those complementary principles of acceptance and restraint will always need working through in multi-racial churches; though the fact that the prohibitions of Acts 15 subsequently lapsed indicates that the details will change. On the one hand there needs to be thorough-going disavowal of any claim to privilege or superiority. On the other hand, there needs to be sensitivity to what different groups – for whatever reason – find offensive. Examples might be the startlingly (for an English person) direct personal questioning that is usual amongst many Asians; or the sort of personal jokes that English people don't find offensive, but others do; or failing to observe the usual standards of punctuality.

Galatians 2:11–16 shows a further stage of the problem, as Paul describes his conflict with Peter over the latter's inconsistency in turning away from table-fellowship with Gentile Christians. The incident illustrates the way prejudice can spread. Peter apparently had no qualms himself about eating with Gentiles; it was pressure from the 'circumcision group' of more traditional Jewish Christians that caused him to hold back. Giving deference to other people's prejudices is always a potent source of discriminatory behaviour. Customers' prejudice was used as an excuse for discriminatory employment policies by banks and shops until it was made illegal; in the early days of West Indian migration, clergy used the prejudices of white members as a reason for discouraging black

---

[8] See Peter H Davids, *More Hard Sayings of the New Testament*, Hodder, 1992, 64.

attendance; white church members can still be cool towards black fellow believers in public because of deference to what other white people think.

Paul's response to such inconsistency was direct confrontation: 'I opposed him to his face, because he was in the wrong' (Galatians 2:11). Colluding with racism justifies it. Fear of 'scenes' or division in church can allow prejudiced behaviour to take the initiative. Paul's grasp of the gospel, and his concern for its clear implementation in practice meant that there could be no compromise with behaviour that actually denied Christian unity.

Elsewhere eating together raised problems that were more to do with social class than ethnic difference, In 1 Corinthians 11 Paul addresses the question of divisions caused by inequality whilst eating the Lord's Supper: 'for as you eat, each of you goes ahead without waiting for anybody else' (11:21). The result is to 'humiliate those who have nothing' (v 22). Such insensitive disregard for the dignity and feelings of the less prosperous is probably what is meant by not 'recognising the body'.[9] It implies that other Christians are – to use a poignant black American phrase, 'no account people'. It is, as we shall see, an experience that black people are all too familiar with, including in our churches, of being treated as 'invisible', as though they weren't there, or don't matter.

Such insensitivity, according to Paul means not only that 'your meetings do more harm than good' (v 17), but even invalidate them as sacraments: 'it is not the Lord's Supper you eat'. (Akin to the way lively 'worship' in Amos 5:21–24 is nullified by acquiescence in injustice: 'I hate, I despise your religious feasts'). To quote Gordon Fee: 'No "church" can long endure as the people of God for the new age in which the old distinctions between bond and free (or Jew and Greek. or male and female) are allowed to persist. Especially so at the Table, where Christ who has made us one, has ordained that we should visibly proclaim that unity.' The belief that we matter and they don't can also he found today, as white people make the same assumptions about blacks. 'Therefore [the worshippers] are not just any group of sociologically diverse people who could keep those differences intact at this table. Here they must "discern/recognize as distinct" the one body of Christ, of which they are

---

[9] See Gordon D Fee, *The First Epistle to the Corinthians*: The New International Commentary on the New Testament, Eerdmans, 1987, 544.

all parts and in which they are all gifts to one another. To fail to discern the body in this way, by abusing those of lesser sociological status is to incur God's judgement'.[10]

It may be significant that most of these ethnic or social conflicts in the New Testament happened in association with food. It is a reminder of how real and material was the fellowship of the early church. Food was important. It is probably true to say that it plays far less of a role in the Church of England than it does in most churches of the world. Most black Christians in Britain will come from backgrounds where eating together is important. What happens when our church eats together can be a fairly good guide to how genuinely multi-racial we are.

---

[10] Fee, op cit, 564.

2. Overcoming Obstacles

We all like being constructive; it is better to build up than to knock down. Yet often, as in Jeremiah's ministry (1:10), the negative needs to precede the positive. The dismal old wall-paper needs to be removed, and the paintwork cleaned up, before the more satisfying and constructive work of decorating can begin. A common failing in all sorts of human enterprises is to neglect the difficult ground-clearing work, and work on inadequate foundations. Only by painful experience do we discover that much well-intentioned effort comes to naught this way.

This is often the case in matters of race. People will say they want to be positive or constructive, and will undertake, and will develop laudable initiatives to develop racial harmony and promote integration. But the essential ground-clearing work has not been done – white racism still festers, and its consequences mean that hard work in the short-term is invalidated in the long-term because this basic issue has not been addressed.[11]

But is it fair to talk of 'white racism'? Most church members would be hurt by the charge that they are racist. Indeed many white people feel like the character in the nightmarish, totalitarian situation depicted in Franz Kafka's novel *The Trial* – imputed with guilt on charges that are never clear by a tribunal that never shows its face. Hostility to the 'race relations industry' stems from this suspicion that it finds white people guilty whichever way they move.

The charge of 'racism' then needs careful unpacking. In the sense that many people understand it, it barely exists in the church today – that is, black people are not openly abused or told that they are not welcome. It

---

[11] The police force likewise illustrates the damage caused by this mistake. Thus the words of Jerome Mack, a black American, responsible for Home Office training of police officers in community relations: '[Police officers] know clear up rates don't come from detection but help from the public, and they are not going to be successful if they are seen as racists or bullies or sexist. There is a cadre who think it is okay to be racist or sexist because in the past the leadership has not been vigorous enough to deal with it'. *The Times* 31/12/1990.

is quite common to meet older black people with that sort of experience, but it has been rare during the past twenty years.[12]

So, what is the problem? A pointer towards it lies in the fact that black participation in Anglican churches is often disappointingly low. Numbers may be quite good in some churches, but they will tend to be weighted to older and more passive people. As one looks towards younger adults; and especially as one looks for greater participation in leadership and responsibility in church life, black participation plummets alarmingly.[13] The disappointed white reaction to this can be simply that 'they' are not interested, and we have done what we can. In fact, there may be quite potent forces at work that discourage black involvement; and when black people feel the freedom to talk honestly, they will begin to point to such factors.

Identifying these negative factors enables us to build a picture of how racism works in a church, and therefore how it can be overcome.

Symptoms of Racism

The following is one classification of some factors in how racism works roughly in ascending order of complexity.

Sheer Racism

As mentioned above ministers nowadays do not suggest to black people that they would rather they did not come next week, but they often don't hear what members of their congregations say. Not that church members are likely to be that rude, but not-so-quiet asides in the pew or on the church steps about the numbers of black people coming can be deliberately calculated to let black people know that their presence is not that welcome. Who knows how widespread such racism is? The black person will probably never come again, and the minister wonder why; the white person probably knows better than to be flagrantly racist in

---

[12] But the experiences still make painful and shameful reading; see for example. the experiences recorded by John Wilkinson in *Inheritors Together*, Board for Social Responsibility, 1985, 14; or Rev Ira Brooks, personal account in *Catching Both Sides of the Wind*, edited by Anita Jackson, British Council of Churches, 1985, 36.

[13] I deal with this at greater length in my article on 'Racism in the Church of England' *Anvil*, No 9, Vol 1, 1992.

front of the clergy. But feed-back from black people suggests that such 'off-the-ball' fouls behind the referee's back are not unknown.

Not Welcoming People

Visitors to churches often comment on the quality of the welcome they received in preference to the quality of preaching, music, or worship. Increasingly it is recognised that a friendly but not intimidating welcome is crucial to a church's growth. It may be that a church's failure to welcome black people simply reflects their weakness in welcoming anyone. A church turned in on itself will grow very little, and certainly not outside its present cultural boundaries. The first time my wife came to church in this country, she was introduced to two committed young Christian women, who said 'Hello' and then continued with their previous conversation.

A poor welcome may simply reflect the lack of social skills and confidence of church members; it may reflect a more vicious estimate of who matters and who does not, of who is welcome and who is not. James recognised the existence of such social partiality in his day (2:1–11); the assumption that black people are 'nobodies', lacking in importance, gifts and value, can be communicated without even being recognised by the communicators.

A development of this, is the refusal of some white members to acknowledge black church members in the street. In various situations I have heard black people comment on it bitterly. It may be shyness, or uncertainty, but at worst it can stem from reluctance to be identified with people whom neighbours might look down upon.

The matter is the more serious because the relational emphasis of most black cultures means that visitors are welcomed with warmth, as a white visitor to a black-led church will discover, and it is natural to show curiosity and interest in strangers.[14] Lack of interest in newcomers may be innocent or malevolent in origin in Anglican churches; it will certainly be lethal for building up a multi-racial church.

---

[14] I remember once being the only white worshipper in a 1000+ congregation in an African cathedral. The preacher apologised to anyone who would not understand him preaching in the vernacular. He was concerned about me!

Refusal to Change

Part of the reason for a tardy welcome to black people may be fear of the changes that may follow. White people can have very inaccurate stereotypes that all black people want noise, tambourines and ecstasy in their worship; although that is very far from the norm of worship in the Caribbean or Asia. More specifically there can be fear of anyone who may disrupt existing power positions.

It would be wrong to prescribe in advance what changes should happen as a church becomes multi-racial in membership, leadership and ethos. It may change very little. Indeed many black people with an Anglican background of high church worship, will expect dignity and formality.

Therefore early morning communion services may have particular appeal to traditionalist overseas Anglicans. As always, the danger of such services is in colluding with 'minimalist participation', which can be particularly attractive to black people who question how far they are welcome in the church. It is important to try to blend respect for a particular, often disciplined, form of spirituality, with weaning people from an individualistic and limited understanding of the Christian life.

My impression is that multi-racial churches cover a very wide range of liturgical practice, and that the more important changes may well not be predictable, though the music will probably become more vigorous even if the hymn book stays the same. The widespread assumption that multi-cultural churches need to be less structured in their worship is not necessarily true; but it is true that there needs to be conviction and sincerity – 'weight' – in whatever form of worship is used.[15]

It is probably a more certain thing to say that the quality of relationships will change. As will be mentioned below, black communities generally express greater warmth and closeness in personal relationships. A church where that is not reflected will almost certainly be restricted to having just a few, more deferential black people on its peripheries.

People certainly need to be prepared for the mental and emotional demands of crossing cultural boundaries. The cost of the privilege of being on the leading edge of social change is that churches become less

---

[15] Multi-cultural worship is covered in much more detail in my Grove Booklet W236 *Worship in a Multi-Ethnic Society.*

cosy and less familiar. Long established church members need to be helped to see the positives in that change. As well as the privilege of working directly at the modern world's need to find reconciliation between races, there is also the survival need of the local church. The faithful labour of past generations in this place will go to waste unless the church rises to meet new challenges to its mission. In rising to meet those challenges there can also be a new discovery that our food is to do the will of him who sent us (John 4:34).

Recognising Gifts

We now move to less readily identifiable areas. Churches may very positively want to offer an open door to black people, yet only make limited progress. In particular they may get quite a high percentage of black attendance, but experience far greater difficulty in drawing people into leadership or a sense of 'owning' the church.

One reason behind this may well be that there is insufficient recognition of what black people have to offer. There is evidence of the effect of stereotyping in education and work – because people are not expected to show certain abilities, those abilities are not recognised or developed. To that extent the stereotypes are self-fulfilling. White people often have clear pictures of what they expect from black people. They will be looking to Afro-Caribbean people to join the choir; they will not be looking to them to become house group leaders. Overall black people will move into the more routine (apart from musical) jobs; not those involving leadership or teaching skills.

It is significant that in the interview with black church members which provides the basis for Maurice Hobbs' stimulating Grove booklet *Better Will Come: A Pastoral Response to Institutional Racism in British Churches* (Pastoral Series 48, 1991), it is the interviewees' experience of being neglected, and abilities for contributing to the life of the church disparaged, which lies at the heart of their grievance. Failure to draw on the spirituality and potential of black people is not the most obvious form of racism, but I believe it is at the root of the church's failure. Weakness at this pastoral and parochial level vitiates any attempt of the church to speak convincingly against racism at a national level.

On a simple level such racism takes the form of just not seeing gifts that are clearly there, if people troubled to find out. My wife came to this country from Malaysia with considerable experience in personal

16

evangelism, building up disciples, and leading Bible studies. Whilst people recognised fairly quickly that she could cook or be hospitable, it was much longer before people recognised these 'word' centred abilities. They did not anticipate them in a non-European.

On a more complex level, gifts may not be recognised because their packaging is unfamiliar. As a very broad generalisation, I believe that black people in Britain are more skilled in human relationships. They share each other's joys and griefs more readily. They are more able to speak the truth to each other in ways that heal. They are more ready to share weaknesses. All of this represents a life-giving resource to the church, that brings death if we neglect it (chapter 4.2 deals with this in greater detail). These are gifts that church leaders may not have sharp eyes for; we have got by for so long without them. Yet they refer to qualities that black people expect from our churches, and they will tend to go elsewhere if they are lacking. Equally they are necessary for the wholeness of the church in Britain. I believe it is not coincidental that the two most effective home groups in our church have black leaders.

Because of the self-fulfilling nature of racist stereotyping, the reality of our situation is that black people in our churches (as with working-class white people) often do not look obvious candidates for leadership. They don't fill out the sort of profile we have as we look for potential leaders. Thus gifts may be dormant; and confidence so lacking that the person rules out himself for much of the time. It is the responsibility of church leaders, therefore, to be particularly alert to potential leaders whose potential is obscured by lack of confidence, educational failure, instability, or simply an unfamiliar accent or way of doing things.

This is the sort of area where care and forethought can make a significant difference. As Maurice Hobbs writes: 'White people with education and training "know the ropes", can speak and write well, and master the complexities of church finance. The professionals can do things more quickly, and don't require so much explanation and that is important when diaries are full' (p 14). Inertia, then, may well perpetuate white leadership. Multi-cultural leadership will only develop as the main leaders take a closer look at their church and give prayer, thought and energy to encouraging leadership from unanticipated quarters.

Faith in the City has brought welcome initiatives to develop both working class and black leadership. Care needs to be exercised that ineffective or inappropriate leaders are not thoughtlessly chosen, but careful and imaginative nurturing of black leadership needs to happen urgently at the local level if the gifts of the black community are to flourish in the Church of England.

Not Accepting Black Leadership

Racism is bound up with power. No peoples in world history have been as powerful as white people of western Europe and North America have been. This experience of power over other peoples developed a sense of superiority, of the rightness of such a situation. Dismantling this sense of superiority is fundamental to overcoming racism, and it is most threatened when it comes to non-whites taking power over whites.

The question of where power lies in the church, then, is of crucial importance. Do black people hold positions which actually enable them to shape the life and activities of the church? This means more than office holding in maintenance areas of church life, such as being a sidesman. It means more than holding official titles that may carry little real weight. Membership of the PCC may in reality mean little; overseeing the church hall kitchen may in reality mean a great deal. There has been much concern about getting black people on to Deanery Synods recently. But do Deanery Synods really affect the life of the Church of England?

Decision makers may well reflect their own assumptions without question. I remember hearing a white lady judge a church youth groups choir competition. Her largely technical comments reflected concerns quite different from those of the black choirs present. Inevitably they felt excluded. The values and needs of black people in the Church of England will only shape policies when black people are in positions of authority, both nationally and locally. This means, it is essential in our churches that white people acknowledge the power of black people to take decisions over matters that affect them, by black people being clergy, wardens, treasurers or on key committees.

In sum, the results of racism are seen in the profile that we in fact have of black involvement in the Church of England. It is much stronger amongst older people than younger – roughly amongst those who were schooled in the Caribbean rather than Britain, which means those more likely to have been born before 1945 than afterwards. Black men are even more likely to be notable by their absence than are white men. Black people who are in our churches are likely to be deferential and ready to accept the status quo of white leadership. Thus, alongside declining participation as one moves down the scale of age, is declining involvement as one moves from occasional attendance through regular commitment to taking up responsibility and eventually leadership.

Overcoming Racism

Some racism is like the clothes we wear, consciously and deliberately chosen. More often racism is like our body odour – something we barely recognise and may even not be aware of, but which is always with us and hard to get rid of. Overcoming racism is therefore a complex and even baffling business. One danger of fierce, public denunciations is that they make identifying and removing racism seem too simple, as though it was simply a problem caused by those who vote for the British National Party. What follows are some of the strategies we need to adopt in trying to chop the heads off the hydra.

By Example

In his confrontation with Peter in Galatians 2 Paul recognised both that racism spreads easily if acceded to, and also diminishes if clearly resisted. Christian leaders need to set a tone of firm opposition to racism. We need to make it clear that we are committed to welcoming people of all backgrounds into every level of our church life; and that the life and leadership of our church will reflect its multi-cultural membership. What David Smith writes of the role of management in industry is equally true of leaders in churches 'Resistance from white workers can be overcome (but not removed) far more easily than might be thought from listening to what prejudiced people say, provided that management and unions are firm enough to create the impression that no scope will be allowed for prejudice to express itself in action ... Perhaps feelings of racial prejudice are taken seriously only where there is still some ambiguity as to whether it is socially acceptable to act on them'.[16]

Clear and firm pressure to have curry at the Harvest Supper; to have a variety of non-British accents reading lessons; to have black people leading home groups or handling the church finances all help to communicate to church members standards of what is expected. So does

---

[16] David J Smith, *Racial Disadvantage in Britain*, Penguin, 1977, 180.

friendliness towards black people and a refusal to make comments with racist under-currents.

By Teaching

Scripture is our great weapon against racism. We need to be alert to the way it bears upon racism, and to help our congregation to read their Bibles with the same awareness. Chapter 1 looked at biblical teaching about the people of God in this light. Biblical exegesis over the past twenty years has become newly aware of how much Scripture has to say about God's concern for justice, his action on behalf of the oppressed, and his concern for the poor. 'Race' is about such issues. At times we may address them directly. It is just as important that our regular preaching picks up such issues: Joseph, the immigrant, had no chance of being heard when accused by Potiphar's wife.

By Confrontation

Does a basically white church become multi-racial by stealth or by open conflict? I know of cases of both. Deciding which strategy to follow is of fundamental importance, and the merits of the different approaches need careful thinking through. Perhaps it depends on both the church and the minister. There are times when a sense of racial superiority is so entrenched that a sharp blow is needed to dislodge it; and some leaders have a taste for conflict. On the other hand we need to be aware that there is often inconsistency between what people say and do: in either direction. Liberal words can shroud racist mentalities. Conversely, racially incorrect remarks can disguise an underlying openness to black people. Then, too sharp a reaction to racist remarks can polarise people, or mean that they learn not to speak their minds.

The lady described by John Rex and Robert Moore will be familiar to many church leaders: 'She associated the rapid deterioration of the area with the arrival of coloured people and expressed the wish that they would go. At the same time she showed quite affectionate regard for her Kittician [from St Kitts] neighbour, with whom she was on friendly terms and whom she helped when a problem arose regarding the transfer of the neighbour's child from one school to another. Miss A has no relatives other than her father. She "keeps herself to herself", devoting most of her life to her father, to keeping the large house in spotlessly good order and working for her parish church'.[17]

It is important that such people are also treated with respect and not scape-goated for problems which go far deeper in our society. Black people often have a humane awareness of why such people are unhappy with the changes that have happened around them. Nonetheless the church needs to acknowledge, confront and repent of the racism in its ranks. Our bishop has on occasions publicly apologised to black people for the coldness and racism that they have met in our churches. I have been impressed at how healing this has been for longstanding black members of our church.

Whilst it is important not to create a sense that a multi-racial community or church will be 'difficult', equally we need to be prepared to face conflicts in building a multi-racial church. Because racist assumptions – very often unconscious and hard to identify – are so deeply entrenched in our society, all sorts of situations can arise where black people are excluded, and where it is not easy to convince white people that exclusion on racist grounds is happening. Yet it needs to be done, by both white and black leaders, if the pattern of black marginalisation in our church is not to persist.

By Encounter

There is no simple one-off solution to removing racism, but constant exposure to relationships with black people that are fruitful and rewarding is a potent solvent of racism. Relationships are at the heart of the Christian understanding of God and of the gospel. For Christians, therefore, racism is ultimately countered by relationships. Commitment to anti-racism can be a barren ideology from which genuine human meeting is alarmingly absent. This is not to deny that there must be concern with countering injustice and prejudice but the gospel's final word is a positive one: 'how good and pleasant it is when brothers (and sisters) live together in unity' (Psalm 133:1). Finding the ministry of black people enriching, working in a team together, learning and contributing, all create an atmosphere of mutuality where racism is exposed as a joyless waste of all that we have to receive and give.

---

[17] John Rex and Robert Moore, *Race, Community and Conflict*, OUP, 1967, 60–61.

But such closeness has to be worked towards. British people can enjoy the ministry of visiting African evangelists yet simply regard it as exotic. More deep-seated change only comes as they are close enough to black people to listen to their experiences and receive their perceptions. I have heard black people testify to how healing they have found this. Would Miss A, in the previous section, have let her 'affectionate regard' for her Kittician neighbour, make her take seriously the latter's experience of racism? Would she allow the anger, or support her demands for equality? It is at this point that the reality of Christian fellowship is tested. It is when we are with black people in identifying the injustices that racism generates and seeking ways to overcome it, firstly in church, but then in people's wider experience, that we are countering racism. True sharing involves both identifying with the pain that others feel, and allowing it to be passed on to yourself. In this way true fellowship is built.

3. Going Forward

There is no blue-print for building multi-racial churches. Such a blue-print would draw us towards techniques and away from people, and ultimately be counter-productive. But there are a number of key areas we need to attend to if the presence of black people in our society is to be reflected in our churches.

Shaping the Ministries

Studies of church life frequently underline the decisive role of the minister in the way the church develops. A church can only be multi-racial if the minister is consciously committed to its being so. In expressing that commitment, the following are particularly important qualities for a minister to work at:

Vision

What was written about convictions in the first chapter needs to be clearly affirmed in the minister's own mind. We need to be convinced that God wills a visible demonstration of multi-racial community in the life of his people. There are voices, notably elements of church growth thinking, which emphasise that people like to be with 'our kind of people' and who advocate that we tailor church life to work along with this need. We need to be clear that this is 'evangelism without the gospel'.

However, we might also question how far the 'homogenuous unit pnnciple' is true in Britain today. Pepsi-Cola and Benetton adverts express young people's desire for multi-racial community. This is reflected in the growth of multi-ethnic, usually young and usually Pentecostal congregations in most large urban areas. At any one time, some aspects of the gospel will be attractive to a society, other aspects will be offensive. So Christians need to be prepared to offend the pluralist mentality of our times by asserting that Jesus is the only Lord and Saviour. Equally we need to take advantage of the attractive potential of a fully multi-racial church in a society that wants to find ways to transcend ethnic conflicts.

Enthusiasm

Surviving in Britain has required black people to develop sharp instincts about whether they are welcome or not. If their presence makes people feel offended, embarrassed, guilty or just insecure, that will be soon sensed; and people will withdraw. Ministry in a multi-racial society demands positive enthusiasm in welcoming and appreciating people of different races. Christian conviction that God is both the creator of all peoples, and that his grace comes to us through other cultures, is a spur to responding positively to people of other races. If 'race' is seen as a problem and an unwelcome and additional source of difficulty in an already over-complex world, then we will unwittingly communicate that negative stance. We should rejoice that every step towards greater ethnic diversity takes us one step nearer to that great multi-cultural richness of worship that Revelation 7 foresees in heaven.

Understanding

Enthusiasm leads to a desire to know. Multi-racial Britain calls for understanding geographically as we seek to develop accurate awareness of the different parts of the globe that people have migrated from in the past 40 years. Historically it requires both some understanding of the centuries-long interaction of Europeans with the rest of the world, which does not gloss over the appalling brutality to be found in slavery, colonial rule and contemporary racism. It also requires understanding of the rapid changes of the past 40 years, both for British society and more especially for communities for whom migration has meant even greater changes.

Thus a good atlas is a basic tool. People deserve to have their background taken seriously. To that needs to be added alertness to what is happening today, and the different ways people respond to life in Britain. Ethnic minority music, films, radio and television can give us clues. Above all, we need simply to listen to people, and take their experience seriously, and not be too quick in trying to force it into the grid of our own understanding.

Affirmation

One of the consequences of racism has been a devaluing of non-whites; added to which a general characteristic of British society is an unhealthy tendency towards criticism and negativity. Affirming that non-white people are both welcome in themselves, and that we expect them to have much to offer, is therefore most important. Public declarations of this, however, may have little mileage in them; white people have spoken with forked tongues too often. The good, old-fashioned work of visiting people in their homes is powerfully affirming, whilst requests to take on some form of service may need frequent repetition for people who are unsure of their welcome.

Listening is an important part of such affirmation. Most of us like to impress, and most black people will be very polite in the presence of a white clergyman and say what is expected. It is vital that clergy give black people the confidence to express their true feelings, including their hurts, about life in Britain, and life in their church. People need to be given space to express themselves. Nor is this true simply with the clergy. In church life as a whole, it is vital that black people can say what white people may not want to hear, and that this is neither curtly dismissed nor patronisingly assented to, but rather seriously weighed.

Flexibility

In all of this we need to recognise that a multi-racial church will change us. At times that will be painful, as we come to terms with our own prejudices, or the hurts that other people feel towards us. At times it will simply be strange, as we eat with our fingers or listen to music we do not understand. At times we will feel out of our depth, as we encounter attitudes to life, belief and morality that do not match what we are used to; at times we will find it greatly enriching. Paul had learned 'to become all things to all men so that by all possible means I might save some' (1 Corinthians 9:23). Such readiness for change must always mark those who would minister cross-culturally.

Some of these things can be taught, some cannot. There is considerable advantage to be gained by giving more training to clergy to minister in multi-racial parishes. There is information that can be communicated, awareness that can he developed, skills that can be passed on, and above all a blend of realism and confidence that can be engendered. Proposals to crowd further the timetables of theological colleges can be unrealistic, but there need to be more opportunities of in-service training for those beginning ministry in multi-racial areas.

Recognising Gifts

A major theme of this booklet is the need to recognise what black people have to give. At the heart of a Christian perception of a multi-racial society, indeed at the heart of our understanding of why God's providence has led to a multi-ethnic humanity, is the conviction that interaction with other cultures develops our humanity – it can lead us towards fulfilling the stature of Christ.

Identifying the gifts that ethnic minorities bring to British society is a fraught business. This is partly because it is often a very subjective question of personal impressions; partly because it can give the appearance of unhelpful rigidity to a situation which is human and flexible; partly because it has often been done so badly in the past: believing that 'West Indians are such happy people with a wonderful sense of rhythm' is a sure way of shutting out any worthwhile black contribution to a church.

It is worth adding that at this point the particularities of the various 'non-white' cultures in Britain become increasingly important. Different cultures will offer differently nuanced gifts. Given these complexities then, here are my impressions of some of the strengths that ethnic diversity can bring to English churches.

Dependence on God

When I was first ordained and prayed with older West Indians, especially women, I noticed that they would often thank God for giving them strength to get through the day. I used to write this off as merely a formula prayer, with little personal meaning. Of course, everyone got through the day! It took several years before it dawned on me how much reality lay behind such a prayer for someone living on the fourth floor with no lift; facing the pressures of hard physical work in an aging body and with little recognition; aware of all the moral pitfalls facing her family; and all this with close relatives too far away to give help in need, or receive help in old age and sickness. Simply receiving the strength to survive was a significant gift from God. In such situations God's blessing on the poor becomes particularly real.

So too I have noticed that in church prayer meetings, black people are often the first to pray and pray with an intensity and urgency that gives an edge to the meeting. The emphasis on technique, on self- sufficiency, on seeming in control, can all dull the edge of dependence on God in western society, and lead to a lukewarm and superficial spirituality.

Accepting Pain

The competence of western society can lead to an over-readiness to solve problems. We can pray for healing for people, not out of compassion for them, but because their pain troubles us. Difficulties are either quickly cleared up or ignored. Many non-Europeans know better that pain has to be faced and lived with – in our bodies, in marriage and other relationships, in the wider society.

In this respect, I believe it is significant that most non-white Christians in Britain take Good Friday much more seriously than white Christians do, for whom church services can simply delay the holiday. The experience of black people often makes them more ready to stand and watch by the cross, not simply to see it as a necessary ingredient in the formula for removing sin, nor an awkward prelude to the celebration of Easter Sunday. For West Indians particularly, centuries of suffering have made their culture far more ready to identify with Christ on the cross, and to ask him into their sufferings. By staying with the pain of the cross, the pain in our lives and in the world, we are more able to have depth and endurance to our faith, and steer clear of a superficial faith which is only able to handle good times. Churches in multi-racial areas are wise to make sure Good Friday is taken very seriously.[18]

Empathy

I have in mind here a whole range of relational qualities which enable people to get closer to each other, and so minister and be ministered to in churches. I would regard it as a far more important attribute of black Pentecostal churches than more obvious differentia such as the singing and tambourines. Correspondingly it is what black people of all backgrounds are most likely to find missing in traditional English churches.

Visiting people when sick, offering practical forms of support, letting people know when they are missed, all tend to be more common amongst black Christians; assuming they have begun to identify with the church they attend. Indeed, there may even be an 'underground' network

---

[18] In my experience, the other occasion on which black people of all backgrounds come to church in particularly high numbers is New Year's Eve. There may be less theological weight in such a practice, but churches ought to make the most of a Watchnight service, and also of the first Sunday in the year.

of black pastoral support in a church community that white leaders are unaware of.

The place where such pastoral support is seen par excellence is funerals; nothing illustrates better the relational differences between black and white than the sparse attendance and reined-in emotions of a white funeral in contrast to the massive attendance and deep expressions of grief at a black funeral. A minister needs to share in such feelings, assist in their expression, and be able to minister Christ's comfort and hope.

However, it would be wrong to see such empathy as limited to the hard experiences of life. For a visitor to a black Pentecostal church the dominant impression may well be one of joy, albeit joy worked out of suffering. In an Anglican church the joy may be expressed differently, but there should still be that underlying warmth that comes from people enjoying being together, and providing support and hope to each other.

How are these qualities fed into a church? People's confidence to be themselves is crucial. In various ways, most black people received Christianity as the religion of a dominant and alien power. So be it – the past is beyond our control. But in the present it is essential that people are able to express their faith in ways true to themselves. Both black Pentecostal and the newer 'international charismatic'[19] churches have grown because they encourage that.[20] How it can happen in an Anglican church is one of the most vital questions we can face. Developing black leaders can be crucial in unblocking the log-jam of unexpressed spirituality in the whole black membership. So can events which express the culture and identity of black members, either within general church events such as fairs or harvest suppers, or events sponsored by particular ethnic groups. Our church has annual Caribbean evenings which spotlight what the culture of the Caribbean offers, though it is essential

[19] I use this phrase to refer to churches such as Kensington Temple or Victory church in London, or many smaller churches, often renewed traditional Pentecostal churches, which have seen considerable growth over the past decade. Typically they will be international (though especially African) in membership, rather than of one culture; and will have a more optimistic eschatology and less rigid behavioural codes than Afro-Caribbean Pentecostal churches.

[20] 'I don't really understand the way white people worship': the words of a female black Pentecostal minister to Adewale Maja-Pearce in *How Many Miles to Babylon?* Heinemann, 1990, 130.

to stress that they are for all church members not just those of Caribbean background.

A controverted question is how far groups for people of particular backgrounds should be regular features of church life. I believe they need to be seen clearly as interim measures, and not to attain such prominence that members are effectively hindered from building relationships with other church members. Given that, they can be useful in building up the confidence of particular minorities in a church, and providing a spring board from which they can make substantial and organised contributions to the life of the church as a whole. For example, we have a monthly Sri Lankan fellowship. Hopefully this is not so demanding that it prevents members participating in other, general church activities, and instead helps those who have felt fairly peripheral in the church's life to feel more at home. It has also been a time when we have been able to plan specifically Sri Lankan contributions to services.

The question of how far people from different ethnic groups are contributing to a church needs constant monitoring. Do they sing with all their heart? Do they readily come forward to serve in various ways? Do they have the sort of confidence in the church that enables them to invite their friends along? All these questions help us see how far black people see themselves as add-ons to an essentially white church, and how far fully participating members of 'a chosen people, a royal priesthood, a holy nation (*ethnos hagion*), a people belonging to God' (1 Peter 2:9).

Spreading the Gospel

What is written above applies mainly to pastoral care of people who visit our churches and keep on coming. In my experience, once a church and its minister are known to be welcoming, people will come and churches will grow without the need for an overt evangelistic strategy. However, we will tend to touch the most 'church inclined' black people, which means older people, especially women, whose roots are in the church overseas. At present this is very largely the limit of the church's effectiveness. By contrast two major groups are largely untouched by the Church of England: young people of Afro-Caribbean background and people of other faith backgrounds.

Afro-Carribean Young People

The slogan that 'the church is always one generation away from extinction' has particular point with the black community. It faces a considerable struggle to see coming generations of British-raised black people joining it.[21] Unless it is able to develop effective evangelistic outreach to this group it will wither as a multi-racial church, and its credibility to address a multi-racial society will be lost entirely.

Given the injustices that young black people suffer from, and the extent to which there can be a real cultural gap to bridge, it is right that the Church of England has generally avoided crass or triumphalistic evangelism amongst black people. But such reticence has tended to mean no evangelism at all. The need is desperate for people who will give themselves to long-term, faithful and unspectacular witness to young black people.

It is easier to outline the problems here rather than the solutions, but at least being clear about the nature and extent of the problem will help us in seeking realistic solutions. As regards its ministry to young blacks there are three areas of difficulty to be overcome.

a) The Church of England is perceived as of a piece with a racist society. Older black people are often used to a more deferential approach to white people. They will put up with things that their children will not. So young people will look at the church more suspiciously. They will see little evidence of black leadership; they may find little instinctive understanding of how black people in Britain live; they can easily bracket the church with other established groups they feel have failed them, such as the police and the education system. There may be exaggeration and misinformation in this (the positive achievements of western missionaries, for example, are often unjustly maligned). Nor should hostility be exaggerated – perhaps it is the generally higher level of religious awareness in the black community that means that the roughest looking young blacks can be impressively well disposed to clergy. Nonetheless, as an institution the Church of England has insufficiently

---

[21] The observation to Renate Wilkinson in *Inheritors Together*, Board for Social Responsibility, 1985, reflects very widespread experience: 'One of the parish priests I interviewed told me that in his experience ministering to the black members of his congregation involved two kinds of ministry, one to the first generation, the other to the second. At the moment we are still learning how to minister to the first generation', 44.

30

distanced itself from the failure of British institutions as a whole to treat black people justly.

In some quarters this reason is seen as the only cause of the problem – thus energy is focussed on overcoming it alone: by the church developing a higher anti-racist profile; by rapidly moving black people into positions of leadership as an encouragement to all black people to believe they have a potential stake in the church; by stressing, perhaps over-stressing, the potential of the young black people that there are in the church. However there are two further aspects to the problem, which if ignored will still make the church's mission ineffective.

b) Young black people hear 'the gospel' in the terms presented by black Pentecostal churches. The generalised understanding of 'becoming a Christian' in the black community is that which has come through the Pentecostal churches. A large proportion of those who have grown up in Britain have been to Pentecostal Sunday Schools. Virtually all black people will have a relative or friend who is a member of one.

Black Pentecostal churches ask for high stakes and offer high rewards. 'Becoming a Christian' means wholescale rejection of a 'worldly' way of life: parties, smoking, drink, make-up, jewellery, promiscuity. The reward for taking up this way of life, which is distinctly unattractive to most young black people, is not only the promise of heaven, but also in this life membership of a strongly supportive community, a sense of self-worth and direction, a life of self-discipline which is seen to bring a measure of material well-being, and opportunities for status and leadership.

But when 'white' churches ask young black people to become Christians it sounds like high stakes and low rewards. Serious Christianity is still taken to have all the negatives listed above – what else can it mean? But set against those demands, the rewards seem paltry. Losing one's old circle of good-timing friends, to feel isolated amongst genteel and distant church people; feeling forever culturally alien in a setting where your gifts are unlikely to be recognised and where leadership and status can seem unattainable. This booklet has in a sense been about how churches can maximise the rewards they offer to young blacks – a sense of community, of affirmation and self-worth. Even more elusive is the task of re-negotiating with black people what are the costs of being a Christian. If Christians can drink beer, listen to reggae and even smoke, then wherein lies the distinctiveness of Christian behaviour? Setting out the inward demands of discipleship in terms of loving relationships, commitment to service and concern for justice needs thoughtful and careful application if it does not sound like a form of insipid, inferior, 'white' Christianity.

c) Black young people are influenced by the culture of their white peers. A black social worker in the 1960s wrote: 'My own view is that no programme aimed at getting more West Indians in church will succeed unless such programmes do something first about church participation by natives of this country'.[22] The past quarter century has borne out the truth of that observation. Despite the stronger recognition that has developed since then of a specific black cultural identity, the point remains vitally important and easily neglected. One should not underestimate the degree of interaction between white and black people – the way in which football has eclipsed cricket as the main sporting interest of black people growing up in Britain indicates the power of traditional urban white norms. Whilst some young black people will have very little contact with whites, many more will interact with varying degrees of ease. At one level, the very deep-seated secularity of young white working-class people, rubs off on blacks. Why create problems by becoming religious, and making yourself unnecessarily different from your white peers?

More profoundly, young working class whites and blacks alike share a very considerable cultural distance from the Church of England – bookish, cool, very rational, as against the vigorous, concrete, congenial culture young whites and blacks share. Thus to see the church's problem as simply that of 'race' is partial – until the Church of England finds ways to overcome its alienation from the non-book based culture of most working class people in this country, it will fail to make significant impact on the black community that is growing up in Britain.

The Church of England, then, faces multiple problems in relation to young, working-class Afro-Caribbean people. It needs to repent of and throw off its racism; it needs to learn to communicate with young blacks; it needs to tackle the massive problem of being and sharing good news with working class Britain. There are no simple solutions or easily

---

[22] In Clifford Hill & D Matthew (eds), *Race: A Christian Symposium*, Gollancz, 1969, 164.

repeatable success stories in this situation Rather, the first step needs to be to recognise the extent of the problem, eschew simplistic solutions, and cry out to God for help, and especially to raise up those who can be effective disciple-makers in this area. *Faith in the City* gave a higher profile to this area of ministry in Britain. It needs to stay in the forefront of prayer and concern, planning and giving. In particular, to make progress there needs to be the long-term dedication of people to minister in this area, and the nurturing and developing of the potential we do have amongst young black people.

Asians of Other Faith Backgrounds

5% of Asians in Britain (that is 80,000) define themselves as Christians.[23] The size of this minority is easily under-estimated, and they can justly claim both pastoral and political neglect. Pastorally, the challenge is not greatly dissimilar to that of Afro-Caribbeans of Christian background, and which forms the substance of this study.

The much greater number of Asians of Hindu, Moslem or Sikh background present a much greater challenge. The propriety of evangelism amongst this group would be denied by some in the Church of England, whilst uncertainty about how to evangelise sensitively but clearly makes the silence more widespread. It would need a book in itself to discuss the propriety of such evangelism. Suffice it to say here that any restriction of the church's evangelistic mandate ultimately invalidates the whole evangelistic enterprise. What theological barriers against evangelising Indians in Britain today would not also have ruled out Columba or Augustine evangelising the Anglo-Saxons,[24] or the early church evangelising Jews or Greeks? If one believes that Jesus Christ is

---

[23] The figure of 5% Christian (3% Roman Catholic, 2% Church of England – sic) comes from Colin Brown, *Black and White Britain – the Third PSI Survey*, Heinemann, 1984, table 2, 24. The 1991 Census gave a British Asian population of about 1,600,000.

[24] One suspects that King Ethelbert of Kent's immediate response to Augustine's preaching – 'Your words and promises are fair indeed; but they are new and uncertain, and I cannot accept them and abandon the age-old beliefs that I have held together with the whole English nation' – would be taken by some Anglicans today as sufficient cause to abandon any evangelistic intention. See The Penguin Classics translation of Bede, *A History of the English Church and People*, 1955, 69.

the good news, then to exclude particular ethnic groups from the scope of evangelism looks like racism.

A potent source of confusion here is the pressure from our society to see religion as merely one aspect of culture – a pressure that our established heritage makes Anglicans particularly vulnerable to. We urgently need to develop the skill of being both vigorously multi-cultural and rigorously mono-religious.[25]

But how is such evangelism to be done? Again, we begin by admitting our uncertainty and sense of impotence. If there is a way ahead, it lies in praying for opportunities, waiting for them, and not being discouraged if they are slow. I like the words of one Asian Christian, Pradip Sudra, about such ministry: 'It is difficult, but not impossible.'

I believe the following principles are important for evangelising people of other faiths in Britain today:

It Takes Time

Clergy need to be prepared to commit themselves for a long period, to get the feel of a community, to be seen as an integral part of it. One young woman from a Hindu background was helped on her journey to faith through being invited to a Billy Graham meeting – nine years after my previous contact with her. By contrast, to expect short-term teams of visitors to be effective evangelistically invites disillusionment, or, worse, a pressure for quick responses that creates long-term problems.

God is Sovereign

People of other faiths do become Christians, usually not through planned strategies[26] (though I do believe that college Christian unions can play a crucial role). It is good to learn to depend on God in a situation we cannot control, and to rejoice as we see him working in unexpected and at times remarkable ways.

---

[25] It is a balance nicely expressed in Zephaniah 3:9 (NIV): 'Then will I purify the lips of the peoples, that all of them may call on the name of the Lord and serve him shoulder to shoulder.'

[26] A similar point is made by David Bronnert based on his experience in Southall in *Sharing Good News*, edited by Patrick Sookhdeo, Scripture Union, 1991, 146–7.

The Church Needs to Look Like Good News

Our presence in a multi-faith community should be welcomed because we are a source of life and love. This can happen in all sorts of ways as Christians share themselves, their energies, their facilities with the local community. Are there signs of the kingdom of God about our churches – whether it be through a playgroup, a holiday club, involvement in local community groups, or whatever particular initiatives are suggested by the local situation?

Our Witness Needs to be Cross-Cultural

There needs to be partnership between Asian Christians and others. Certainly Asian Christians will have advantages of greater closeness to other Asians (though bearing in mind the enormous differences there can he between people from different parts of the sub-Continent – my wife being Malayalee cuts little ice with local Gujeratis; in fact, it is culturally much more relevant in relating to Sri Lankan Tamils). However, it is easy to overlook the often greater impact that the friendship of indigenous English people can have. It is tragic how little interest and welcome most Asian people have had from English neighbours. English Christians who buck this trend, and show warmth and concern, will stand out. It is vital they are helped to value the role they can play through ordinary, everyday concern.

People Need to See a Multi-Cultural Church

It will be very hard for an all-white church to look like a credible spiritual home to non-Christian Asians. Whilst I would question the homogenous unit claim that 'people like to become Christians amongst their own kind of people', I think the principle can legitimately be put in the negative: 'people don't like to become Christians amongst some other kind of people'. Understandably it looks like an unreasonable demand to surrender their cultural identity. A vigorously multi-cultural church makes it clear that such unevangelical demands are not being made. If all sorts of cultures abound in the church, then even if there is no one from their particular group, it should be clear that one more culture will be welcomed.

Responsiveness to the Gospel Varies Between Groups

I think this is a more legitimate conclusion of church growth thinking.

It does not mean we should abandon witness where an ethnic group is not yet responsive; it means we should patiently wait a better day amongst them whilst also focussing on people who are more ready to receive the gospel. For example, the Sri Lankan Tamil refugees who have come in substantial numbers to our area in the past decade, are easier to relate to than the more long-standing Gujeratis. This may be because there are already more Christians amongst them, and a strong tradition of Christian mission schools, and they have not had time to build up the strong, and often gospel-resistant, networks that Gujeratis have.

Overall, I picture the gospel spreading in a multi-racial area rather like ripples in a pond. The first impact has been on people with strong sympathies to the church and of Christian background, notably older West Indian people, especially women. Then younger black people and black men have become more involved. As the church has become multi-racial, we have attracted more Asians of Christian background. We are now beginning to spread across to people of other faith backgrounds, notably Hindu Tamils. I believe that will make it more likely that other Hindus, and then Moslems, will become Christians.

Developing Leadership

This has been identified in this booklet as a major issue facing the Church of England. How can it be done?

By Valuing Young Potential Leaders

Traditionally, Anglican leaders came from the same sources as other leaders of established institutions, notably good public schools and prestigious universities. Not many black people will be found in such places. However, some young black people are 'high flyers' in terms of their faith and commitment to God. Numbers may not be large, but that makes it the more important to give time and care to young people in our churches who show long-term potential for leadership. Such laying of foundations takes time – in teaching the basic spiritual disciplines of prayer and Bible-reading, of starting to share opportunities for ministry and leadership, of openness and hospitality. But present-day leaders can give no greater contribution to the future of a multi-racial church than young black Christians who have been discipled to be future leaders.

By Valuing People Rather Than Programs

I have suggested that black communities in Britain are characterised by greater warmth and empathy than the white community. These are important Christian qualities; yet the increasingly 'managerial' emphasis in the ordained ministry in Britain downgrades them. Typically in inner-city Britain the black-led churches are much worse organised and better attended than the mainstream ones. Good organisation is the servant of people and not to be despised; but we should be especially cherishing and nurturing people in our churches who have gifts in relationships, and the capacity for relationships that kindle faith and discipleship.

A multi-racial church needs multiple leadership. This is not only because it is important that different ethnic groups are enabled to identify more easily with the church's leadership, but because a wider variety of strengths and attitudes needs to be found in the leadership than can ever be found in one person. Leadership with an eye to strategic long-term planning needs blending with leadership that is sensitive to people's need for affirmation and belonging. There needs to be a leadership group that is a model to the whole church of the blending of different cultural emphases.

By Valuing the Emotional as Well as the Cerebral

The Church of England tends to pride itself on being 'a thinking person's church' – and it shows! We ought not to despise the cerebral, but we have woefully failed to cultivate the visceral. A rational account of the Christian faith – God become man for our salvation – ought to be emotionally powerful. Otherwise, either there is something wrong with our reasoning (perhaps we do not really believe it), or we are failing to let our thoughts touch our emotions. The distance from head to heart is often less great for black people. Worship and preaching ought to move people. Most black Pentecostal preachers do this, not usually through manipulation but through conviction. Fear of people who raise the emotional temperature of our churches can freeze out potential black leaders.

By Valuing Indigenous Leadership

Culture does matter. That has long been recognised in overseas mission. It needs recognising in Britain. Quite simply, a Christian leader who shares the culture of his community is advantaged over one who does not. Therefore it is right to seek out black and working class leaders, and to give weight to their identity with the local community. Clergy from outside may have their place but there will always be an element of 'translation' in what they do (though, as mentioned above, they need to work hard at becoming fluent in the local culture of wherever they are). If pastoral experience, personal maturity and academic ability are seen as plus factors in assessing leadership potential, so no less should a person's capacity to communicate readily with his peers. We need local leaders.

By Recognising the Pressures of Life

'Pressure' is (or perhaps was) a keyword in the Afro-Caribbean community. It refers to all that makes life difficult – problems at work, with the family, finance, police, or whatever: and the way that racism intensifies and complicates all those factors, to make life heavy and depressing. Most black people experience greater pressure than most white people do. Life often does not run as smoothly. The gospel may help people cope with pressure, it does not remove it. Potential black leaders, as with many working class potential leaders, may be under pressures that can inhibit their leadership. It is important not to let these things disqualify, and look instead for problem-free leaders. We may look a long time. The limitations that such pressures bring, for example of time, need to be recognised; but so do the strengths. It is often out of their vulnerability and suffering that people minister most powerfully to others. People need to be allowed to work from their wounds.

By Not Leaving People Isolated

When black footballers first began to appear in the Football League in the late 1970s, they tended to appear in clusters of two or three in clubs rather than on their own. I believe that is significant. People feel very exposed in unfamiliar environments. Black people who are moving into leadership in churches may experience prejudice from some quarters. They may be very sensitive to rejection or criticism. If possible, encouraging black leadership in twos or threes provides support and colleagues to share experiences with. For example, the first black members of a PCC may be quiet and passive. As numbers build up, they may well grow in confidence to participate freely and honestly.

Pitfalls

Having said the above, it is worth pointing out some dangers of developing black leadership. It can be done with insufficient awareness of the black community. In particular, it is good that efforts are being made centrally in the Church of England to encourage black leadership, but that is an area where on-the-ground experience can be scarce and policies adopted that are well-meaning but inappropriate. The following dangers await the unwary:

a) Being unaware of distinctions within the black community. The usefulness of 'Black' as a portmanteau term for all non-whites in Britain is a controverted question. It is useful in drawing attention to the common experience of racism. Its weakness is to obscure massive differences of culture, social status and religion. Quite simply, most 'black' people would not see being 'not-white' as the most important thing about their identity.

Proposals to develop 'black' leadership in the Church of England, therefore, risk the danger of being unsubtle. No-one assumes that being white makes me acceptable as a leader to all other whites in Britain. So we need to ask of black people, as we do of whites, how they relate to a particular community, and not simply assume that all black people will easily identify with any black person who is put in a leadership position. One obvious differential is social class and education. A large majority of black people in Britain are working class, and with relatively few qualifications; the majority of black people in and around leadership positions in the Church of England share the middle-class and bookish ethos of the Church of England as a whole. It is insulting to black people to assume that there will be a natural affinity across class and educational background simply because of the colour of people's skin. Certainly, being members of a discriminated against minority provides some common identity, in a way that being white does not, but the significance of that experience needs weighing against other important factors.

A more readily identifiable factor is ethnicity. Obviously there are major cultural differences between 'black' people of Asian and West Indian backgrounds; but there are also more fine-brushed differences within those communities. For example two-thirds of West Indian migrants to Britain came from Jamaica; the majority of Afro-Caribbeans near to leadership in the Church of England are of other island background. A 'typical' Jamaican is not the least similar to a 'typical' Barbadian. West Indians know this; a church that does not, squanders its credibility. I am aware that whites can use such differences malevolently: to 'divide and rule', to classify people like specimens, to be blind to people's ability to transcend boundaries. Nonetheless I believe that the Church of England's effectiveness is reduced by not being aware of distinctions that black people are aware of. Black leaders in the Church of England are usually from middle class and often ethnically untypical backgrounds. We should at least be aware that those we expect to be black leaders are most often not from the majority, working-class, and 'core' ethnic communities, and allow for that in our policies.

b) Focussing on the wrong level of leadership. Most Anglican discussion about black leadership has focussed on producing black ordinands, and then black people in senior church posts; and increasing the number of black people on Synods. There is value in this, but it is not the major issue. I have already stressed that the major challenge facing the Church of England is its failure to reach the core working-class black communities, especially the young. Until we see disciples and then leaders coming from this community, when all is said and done we will still not be a genuinely multi-racial church. At present, seeking greater black representation for black Anglicans at clergy and synodical level is spreading a lot of jobs amongst a rather small group of people, who, as we have seen, largely share the middle-class ethos of the Church of England.

Energy needs to be put into developing black youth leaders, home group leaders, readers and the like, who share the culture of the majority of their community. As ordinands emerge from this group, we will see substantial advance – ministers whom black communities instinctively identify with. However, significant numbers of ordained black leaders will only be found at the far end of a long-term process of serious pastoral work amongst black people. Taking shortcuts, in the attempt to make a good impression by quickly recruiting and promoting black clergy, will misfire.

c) Unthinking use of the concept of 'role models'. This has been a cause of mischief, in that it seems to be assumed that 'role modelling' can be controlled, and only happens positively, as when black people are moved into leadership positions. But role modelling has greater limitations and greater dangers than is commonly recognised. It needs to be realised, firstly, that the most powerful role models are parents. Children, particularly boys, who have not had a model of a caring or responsible father, suffer from a disadvantage that is not easily remedied. Secondly, role modelling happens constantly, negatively as well as positively, in a myriad of ways that cannot be controlled or channelled. I remember hearing some sociologically-trained black youth leaders speak of the need of their members for positive role models, whilst quite oblivious to the way they were themselves modelling incompetence and inefficiency to their members. Black leaders in our churches can be very significant models to the whole community, but only as they minister effectively.

Being Together

How can different cultures thrive within the one church? There are different ways in which cultures can live together in the one Christian community.

1. By blending. In some areas of church life, different cultures can be expressed together with very little difficulty, given an atmosphere of giving way to each other. An obvious example is music. Churches which restrict themselves to one type of music will tend to restrict themselves to one type of person. Increasingly, churches are seeing the need to blend together different types of music – traditional hymns, charismatic choruses, Taize chants, music of various ethnic backgrounds – not only to reflect the tastes or cultures of church members, but also because they express different aspects of spirituality that we need to draw upon.

Hopefully, a multi-cultural church will be able to express different cultures in the one service, with members at times drawing on their own traditions, at times learning to appreciate the traditions of others.

2. By offering alternatives. At times we will all do the same thing together, even if we vary what we do – presumably everyone sings the same hymn tune at any one time! But in other ways people should be free to express individual preference and so contribute to variety. Dress is an obvious example here. It is sad if there is pressure on people to dress for church meetings in a particular way. As well as formal and informal, hopefully churches will foster different ways of dressing that are appropriate for people – so that saris or African robes appear alongside western dress, including quite formal clothes if preferred by some people.

Similarly, when food is served at church occasions, it ought to cover the whole range of cultures expected, and indeed to be weighted towards encouraging minority groups to see that they belong, by taking care to provide their type of food. So people who plan harvest suppers need to be encouraged to draw in Asian or West Indian food as well as whatever has been traditional. In this way people can both see that their culture is valued, and take steps towards enjoying what other cultures offer.

3. By parallels. At times, people can choose to do different things at the same time. The same hymn tune can be sung in different languages together. Or a sermon can be translated. Indeed, if people who do not share a common language are to worship together, something like this must be done.

Knowing when to offer parallels, particularly in terms of language, is a fine judgement. Our church has bi-monthly Tamil-English services at present, because there are a considerable number of Tamil speakers in the area, very largely Hindus who would be quite untouched by an English-language service. On the other hand, whilst a good number of Urdu speakers come to our church, of Christian background, the potential for separation in starting an Urdu-language service have seemed to outweigh the benefits though we may well think differently in future.

There are factors that need to be borne in mind on either side. On the one hand 'mother tongue' services can be of value, even where people have a reasonable command of English, because they use, to quote a Tamil pastor, 'the language of the heart'. Church services are not just for communicating information, they are for worship, communion and self-expression, and worship in one's first language may reach depths that English-language worship fails to reach. On the other hand, there are pitfalls to be aware of. The next generation, educated and more at home in English, may find them tiresome and alien. They run the risk of becoming backward-looking or exclusive, where the main focus becomes cultural identity rather than Christ. As with other things in church life, they can be hard to start but even harder to stop.

4. By making choices. In some areas of life, however, a choice simply has to be made to do things either in one way or another. For practical reasons compromises and alternatives are not possible. You can easily use different styles of music in a church; you cannot easily follow different standards of time-keeping.

The advertised 11 am service, may begin quite definitely within a minute or two of the stated time each week, or people may start to arrive at 11.10, the music begin a few minutes later, and the minister finally enter and welcome people some time around half past. You may choose something between those two approaches but attempting to alternate between them will produce chaos. Only one standard of punctuality can prevail, and churches have to choose which they will adopt.[27]

The point is that, for practical rather than ideological reasons, uniformity is necessary in some matters, of which time-keeping is an example. Whilst in other areas variety is quite possible and indeed desirable, there are issues over which churches need to decide a common policy which is clearly known and recognised.

---

[27] A parallel is pointed to by my irritation with charismatics who invite everyone in a service to worship in the way they feel comfortable: it sounds free and democratic, but in a service of 100 people, if 30 worship as charismatics and 70 do not, the result is charismatic worship. Likewise, a Quaker service only works if everyone agrees to operate by the same rules.

CONCLUSION

This study has arisen both out of certain convictions about the nature of the church and the way we should live in a multi-racial world; and of practical attempts to express that in a local church. There will never be a time when we can say we have arrived. Certainly, the growing ethnic diversity of our own church has been a great encouragement. (Last Sunday, English, Pakistani, Jamaican, Swiss, Japanese, Guyanese Indians and Nigerians all took a significant part in the service). We have seen prejudice and barriers broken down; tensions weathered to produce greater understanding, growing diversity in leadership. And quite simply, a multi-racial church is, in itself, a strong witness to the local community. On the other hand, we still have very far to go in evangelising people of other faiths, and young black people, especially men. I think white people have not entered very far into the pain and rejection experienced by blacks. I am not fully clear whether or not our worship ought to change to reflect our multi-cultural variety.

However, it is encouraging to sense considerable consensus with others who have written on this field.[28] I believe there is a continuing need to share notes and monitor progress. Increasingly, Christians have the privilege of being part of a gloriously variegated world church. We rejoice in that, and in its growth. But closer inspection always reveals blemishes and imperfections as well. The church in Britain is simply another part of that church, increasingly needing to reflect similar variety and see similar growth. As we are able to see the varied cultures of modern Britain come together in Christian love and unity, we will be making a powerful witness to our society, and carrying forward the purposes of God.

---

[28] See, for example, David Bronnert's chapter on 'Building a Multi-racial church' in *Sharing Good News*, op cit, 130–149; or John and Renate Wilkinson's contribution in *Inheritors Together*, op cit.

Suggested Futher Reading

Malcolm Patten - Leading a Multi-cultural church – SPCK- 2016
Excellent, covers all the ground. Sure-footed and warm-hearted.

Patricia J Williams – Seeing a Colour Blind Future – Virago – 1997
Superb book on experiencing racism by a black legal academic/journalist.

Ben Lindsay – We need to talk about race – SPCK -2019
Personal and discerning account of black experience in white majority churches.

Patty Lane - Crossing Cultures – IVP/USA – 2002
Illuminating introduction to doing what the title says.

Jayson Georges and Mark D Baker – Ministering in Honor-Shame Cultures – IVP Academic – 2016
Introduction to a major cross-cultural difference.

E Randolph Richards & Brandon O'Brien – Misreading Scripture with Western Eyes – IVP Books – 2012
A vital tool in ministering cross-culturally.

J Daniel Hays – From every People and Nation; a biblical theology of race – Apollos/IVP – 2003
Detailed and thorough overview of the biblical material.

Bruce Milne - Dynamic Diversity– IVP – 2006
Theological advocacy of ethnically mixed churches, but says nothing on racism.

Recently Released by the Latimer Trust

A Basic Christian Primer on Sex Marriage and Family Life by Martin Davie

We live in an age in which there is widespread confusion about matters to with sex, marriage, and family life not only in society at large, but also within the Christian Church.

The purpose of this new Primer is to address this confusion by providing clergy and laity alike with a basic introduction to what the Christian faith has to say about these matters. It is particularly designed to help Christians to understand the issues that will be discussed in the Church of England following the publication of the Living in Love and Faith material in late 2020.

The Primer explains in clear terms the basis of a Christian approach to these matters, and then goes on to look at what Christianity has to say about marriage, singleness, friendship, intersex and transgender, sex outside marriage (including same-sex relationships), divorce and re-marriage, birth control and treatment for infertility.

Thomas Cranmer: Using the Bible to Evangelize the Nation by Peter Adam

We need not only to do evangelism, but also develop contemporary gospel strategies which we trust, under God, will be effective. We need gospel wisdom, as well as gospel work. We need to work on local evangelism, but also work on God's global gospel plan. This alerts us to our own nation, as well as other nations. Gospel strategy includes the question, 'How should we evangelise our nation?'

Thomas Cranmer, Archbishop of Canterbury 1532-56, strategised and worked to do this from the perspective of Anglican Reformed theology and practice. We cannot duplicate his plan in detail, but he can inspire us, and also teach us the key ingredients of such a plan. His context of ministry had advantages and disadvantages! Our context has the same mixture. We can also learn from Cranmer's ability to work effectively in his context, despite the many problems, and the suffering he endured. God used him to evangelise his nation at his time. May God use us for his gospel glory!

Focus on Jesus: Handel's Messiah by Robert Bashford

This book provides a commentary on the message of Messiah. Handel's great oratorio gives a marvellous portrayal of the Person and Work of Jesus Christ: the anticipation of his coming, his birth, his ministry, his sufferings and death, his resurrection and his ascension – plus also the proclamation of the Gospel to the world, and Christian assurance of resurrection life beyond death.

The main focus of this study is the selection of Bible verses that make up the work, compiled by the librettist Charles Jennens. At the same time there is also a certain amount of comment on the music, showing how Handel's distinctive skill contributes towards clearly expressing the message.

The aim of the book is that readers may deepen their understanding of the Bible passages included in the work and enjoy Handel's Messiah all the more – and as a result know Christ better.

Come, Let Us Sing. A call to Musical Reformation by Robert S. Smith

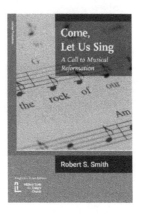

Come, Let Us Sing seeks to help us reform the musical dimension of church life by bringing biblical clarity to two key questions: Why do we come together? and Why do we sing together?

In answer to the first, Robert Smith navigates a path through the contemporary 'worship word wars', concluding that we gather both to worship God and to encourage others. Two questions must, therefore, be asked of everything we do: Does it glorify God? and Does it edify others?

As to why we sing, Smith unpacks three principal functions of congregational singing in Scripture – as a way of praising, a way of praying and a way of preaching. In so doing, he explores the necessity of singing scriptural truth, the value of psalmody, the place of emotions, the role of our bodies, and how singing expresses and enriches our unity.

Come, Let Us Sing is a timely call for the church to reclaim its biblical musical heritage and reform its musical practice.

The Anglican Ordinal: Gospel Priorities for Church of England Ministry by Andrew Atherstone

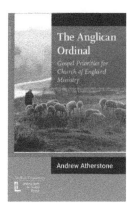

This book is part of our *Anglican Foundation* series, which offer practical guidance on Church of England services.

There is no better handbook for Anglican ministry than the Anglican ordinal – the authorized liturgy for ordaining new ministers. The ordinal contains a beautiful, succinct description of theological priorities and ministry models for today's Church. This booklet offers a simple exposition of the ordinal's primary themes. Anglican clergy are called to public ministry as messengers, sentinels, stewards, and shepherds. They are asked searching questions and they make solemn promises. The Holy Spirit's anointing is invoked upon their ministries, with the laying-on-of-hands, and they are gifted a Bible as the visual symbol of their new pastoral and preaching office. This booklet is a handy primer for ordinands and clergy, and all those responsible for their selection, training, and deployment.

Lightning Source UK Ltd.
Milton Keynes UK
UKHW011235030321
379700UK00001B/241